HOW TO TRAIN YOUR
SUPERHERO

HOW TO TRAIN YOUR
SUPERHERO

DR. RJ JACKSON
ILLUSTRATIONS BY KOREY SCOTT

Published by SmileInOut, Austin, Texas
drrjjackson.com

Edited and designed by Girl Friday Productions
www.girlfridayproductions.com

ISBN (paperback): 978-0-578-68084-2
ISBN (ebook): 978-0-578-77639-2

First edition

For Jeremiah and Isaiah

CONTENTS

———

INTRODUCTION

Hello, the name is Captain Smile, and I am a superhero! More specifically, I am Dr. RJ's superhero. I am here to teach you how to train your superhero. Training your superhero is serious business. You have to be tough. You have to be focused, and you have to be dedicated.

Before we start, it's best that you get to know me a little better. You see, Dr. RJ and I are in the smile business. Doc is an orthodontist. Yep, he is the braces guy. In our partnership, he has the easier job. All he has to do is create perfect smiles. I actually have to make his patients smile—and I'm not talking about using jokes. Dr. RJ spends several months creating a perfect smile so that his patients can be healthy, confident, and happy. The problem is that many use their smile only during times of extreme fun but not on a regular basis. Doc not only wants his patients to have a perfect smile, he also wants each one of his patients to experience true happiness. That's where I come in.

Did you know babies smile more than four hundred times a day but adults smile fewer than twenty? Babies experience true happiness, but as we get older, sometimes our happiness gets less. Have you ever counted how much you smile each day? I am willing to bet that it is nowhere close to four hundred times.

Dr. RJ and I have been working together for years and years, so I'm proud to say that, even though he's a grown-up, he's learned to smile like a baby.

Has anyone taught you about the meaning of happiness? My guess is *no*. There are movies and songs about happiness. In fairy tales, the end goal is to "live happily ever after." If happiness is such a big part of life, doesn't it seem odd that no one has taught you about it? I mean, you learn math, science, and history, but no one is teaching you and your friends about the one thing that everyone in your world wants: happiness.

Well, have no fear, Captain Smile is here! I will teach you all you need to know about happiness. So allow me to adjust my mask and pick up my chalk because class is in session.

CHAPTER 1

WHAT IS HAPPINESS?

I'm sure you are thinking to yourself, "I know what happiness is. I'm happy when I am eating ice cream, playing video games, and hanging out with my friends. Duh. I don't need a superhero to know that." Well, before I tell you the real meaning of happiness, first I must share with you what happiness is NOT.

Happiness is NOT getting what you want when you want it.

Many people believe happiness is all about getting what you want. It feels good to hear the word "yes." It's natural to want things to go your way. But happiness is much more than getting what you want.

What is so awesome about true happiness is that it is always available. It is not based on someone else telling you *yes* or *no*. Why do you think that is?

Imagine if you asked if you could eat cake for breakfast, cookies for lunch, candy for a snack, and ice cream for dinner, and your mom said *yes*. Do you think you would feel happiness when you went to bed? No, your upset stomach would cause you to feel regret. You see, sometimes the word "no" can actually make you happy, simply because the word "yes" would have caused you pain. And sometimes getting what you want can cause you to be unhappy later.

Happiness is NOT having a happy moment while causing others to be unhappy.

Do you have any bullies at your school? Even though they may smile, they don't really feel good inside. Bullying is a clear sign of unhappiness. Every human wants attention. Whether it's attention with good intentions or bad intentions, it is still attention (wow, that's a tongue twister). Bullying is an example of gaining attention with bad intentions.

There could be many reasons why a kid becomes a bully. Maybe they are not getting enough attention at home, so at school they force attention their way. Maybe they believe bullying gets them more attention than what they would get by being nice. Maybe they do not know other ways of getting attention. Whatever the reason, these kids are not experiencing happiness. When people are truly happy, they want everyone around them to be happy as well.

Bragging is also a sign of unhappiness. You know why now: Bragging is seeking attention with negative intentions. And

although you may not notice right away, bragging can make others feel unhappy, and the bragger is typically trying to hide their own pain by faking happiness.

On social media, it seems like everyone is bragging. Everyone wants to show off, especially when it comes to selfies. Do you think taking a photo with filters comes from good intentions? No, kids use filters to enhance their looks. If they think their looks need to be changed, that suggests they aren't happy with the way they actually look. Someone who feels the need to brag or show off is desperate for attention. They just haven't realized that there are better ways to get it.

Examples of ways to get attention with good intentions are giving compliments, doing something nice for someone, or being genuinely interested in what another person has to say. By giving others attention, it's only natural that you will get attention back. And that is the kind that will make everyone happy.

I see that you are not convinced. (Of course I can see that, I am a superhero.) Okay, I have an experiment for you. Pick a person in your class who you would like to be your friend. That's someone you'd like attention from, right? The next time you see them, give that person a compliment and maybe share something about them that inspires you. (Obviously, this needs to be sincere or this could be attention with bad intentions.) Then sit back and watch the magic.

Now that you know what happiness is NOT, allow me to define what it truly is. It may be surprising to know that happiness has everything to do with how you think. . . .

4

The definition of happiness is the state of receiving or creating positive thoughts.

That's right. It is all about how you think.

Look at this example: Two kids move to a new school. One kid is excited about the adventure and looking forward to meeting new friends. The other kid is mad and angry about having to leave his old school. So, did the event of moving to a new school cause the kids to feel a certain way? Or was it the kids' *thoughts* that caused them to feel a certain way? One thinks positively about the move, the other thinks negatively. One experiences happiness and the other experiences unhappiness.

Let's look at another example, this one in sports. Two kids do not make the team. One is disappointed at first but decides to practice harder and is excited to try again next year. The other kid is mad and vows to never play the sport again. Did the *event* of not making the team cause their responses? Or did the *thoughts* about not making the team cause their responses?

It is all about your thoughts.

Thoughts are constantly going in and out of your mind. When your thoughts are positive, you feel happy. When your thoughts are negative, you feel unhappy.

Think of a party with twenty people. Everyone is having a great time. Some people are dancing. Some are eating, and others are talking and laughing. Then three more guests arrive. One is mad, one is jealous of another person, and the last one starts to gossip right away. What do you think will happen to the party?

Even if more happy people show up, the party will not be as fun because of the few negative people.

That is how your mind works.

You could also think of it like your sock drawer. Imagine you put dirty, old smelly socks in your drawer every day for a month. Eventually your entire room will stink. Even though your other clothes are clean, the whole room smells bad. That is how it works in your mind. If you are constantly having negative thoughts, then your entire mind will be negative. This negative thinking will lead to a shift in your brain functioning, which will cause you to be unhappy. It's my job to help keep your thoughts positive and your brain stink-free!

HAPPINESS IS SIMPLE, YET DIFFICULT.

CHAPTER 2

WHY HAPPINESS?

Happiness is one of the most desired goals. Kids want to be happy. Adults want to be happy. Teens want to be happy. Old people want to be happy. Even cats want to be happy, I think. Everyone wants to be happy because of the "feel good" feelings that occur when chemicals such as dopamine and serotonin are released in the brain. Those two chemicals cause you to feel good and can even be quite addictive. But what if I told you that happiness is not only a want but also a need? Allow me to explain.

You see, we superheroes believe that humans are special, that each one of your kind is unique. Just look around to know we're right: you are the only you who exists in the world. That's the definition of unique!

It's surprising how humans will pay so much money to buy an original famous painting or the rarest gem but might treat the rarest human like trash. Too often, humans put high value on objects that are rare but ignore living, breathing people who are rare.

Superheroes believe that every human was created with a purpose and for a purpose. This should not be hard to believe. If every creature, no matter how big or small (even a roach) has a purpose, it shouldn't be hard for you to believe that you have one. (You're far more advanced than a roach—and less disgusting too!) We superheroes are here to remind you just how special you are.

Humans need to be unique. This is so each one of you can do the things in your world that only you can do.

Have you ever been part of a team before? You probably noticed that every team member is completely different (despite the uniforms). Each person has a special skill, which helps the team succeed. That is the reason there are different positions in sports, different roles in theater, and different instruments in a band. When all the team members use their skills together, they produce something amazing.

This same idea applies to you in your world. Each human is completely different. You are the right size, the right height, the right age. You have the right sense of humor, the right intelligence, the right level of courage, the right amount of influence, the right personality, and so on, just as you are right now. You're you, the only person you can be!

Although you are unique, there are parts of you that are similar to other humans. For example, even though you have many differences, you may be the same height, have the same eye color, make the same grades, and play the same sports as your friend. Those similarities can make it easier to help each other.

Imagine if your parents have been divorced for a few years. Do you think you will be able to help a friend who is going through their parents' separation more than someone whose parents are together? Yes. Since you have been through it, you are able to connect on a different level.

Each event in your life and each part of your personality adds to your story, and no matter where you are in your story, you have the ability to positively impact someone else. If you have been bullied, then you can truly connect with someone who is getting bullied. If you did not like your appearance, then you can truly connect with someone who dislikes their appearance.

As superheroes, we know that often the things you might dislike about yourself the most are the very things that connect you to others. Think about a puzzle. Imagine if the corner piece dislikes the fact that it has two sides with curves. Guess what? The curves are what connect the puzzle piece to other pieces.

Dr. RJ had a patient once who felt that her ears were too big. Kids used to make fun of her. But after she learned to train her superhero, she began to appreciate her appearance. In fact, she started a blog about accessories where she posted pictures of herself wearing different types of earrings. She didn't try to hide her ears. Now her ears help her connect with people all over the world. Your uniqueness can be a tool to bring joy and happiness to the world daily.

Happiness is contagious, and when you use your unique self to spread happiness, you become a part of something truly amazing. Think about spreading a cold. One person with the virus coughs in their hands, then high-fives a friend who rubs his nose, then that friend shares a drink with a teammate, then that teammate hugs and kisses her mom, and so on. Happiness works the same—but in a good way! You learn how to train your superhero, then you positively influence your friends, who positively influence their classmates, who positively influence their teammates, and so on.

This is why happiness is so important. Sure, it is nice to feel good and have happy moments, but happiness is bigger than that. Happiness allows you to be who you were created to be. Happiness allows you to positively impact those around you in a special way. Happiness allows you to be nice and considerate. It allows you to be courteous and obedient. Happiness allows you to be giving, caring, and kind to others.

Happiness is powerful enough to change the mood of someone who is unhappy. The next time your parent comes home from work and you can tell it wasn't a good day, try this. Give a smile and a hug and say, "I love you." Chances are you will lift everyone's mood.

But what if you are unhappy yourself? When people are unhappy, they focus only on themselves. It is a natural reaction. It would be hard for you to lift the spirits of someone else if you were too busy with your own unhappiness. Superheroes see this all the time.

Say you made a mistake and your parents grounded you. Instead of having positive thoughts, such as examining how to improve what you messed up, you focus on negative thoughts. But you will be spending your immediate future grounded no matter what thoughts are in your head; why waste that time on negativity when you could still find a way to feel happiness?

One of my superhero friends told me about an intense battle he had. His human side was upset with his parents because they took away his phone for a month. He felt that his parents were being cruel. My friend had a tough battle, but in the end, he won. He finally apologized to his parents and used his extra free time to practice writing. Every time he had the urge to text his friends or get on social media, he would write instead. The last I heard, he was writing uplifting poems for the elderly in nursing homes, spreading happiness.

When you are unhappy, you forget that you are special and unique and that only you can impact others in your own special way. Happiness is not only a want. Your mom, your dad, your friends, your teacher, and even strangers NEED you to be happy.

EVERYONE NEEDS YOU TO BE HAPPY.

CHAPTER 3

THE WHEN, WHERE, AND WHO OF HAPPINESS

WHEN should you be happy?

You should be happy when eating vegetables, and you should be happy when there's no dessert. You should be happy while washing dishes and while sitting quietly in class. You should be happy while making your bed and while doing homework. You should be happy when the swimming pool is closed, and you should be happy when you ask for something and the answer is *no*. You should be happy when your parents take away your phone, and you should be happy even if no one likes your selfie on social media. You do not have to get stuck in negativity until the fun and exciting moments occur. You can be happy whenever you choose.

Allow me to show off my superhuman wisdom: The more you are happy, the less you are unhappy. So choose happiness.

CHOOSE HAPPINESS.

WHERE should you be happy?

Your superhero is always with you. Wherever you go, your superhero is right there. Your superhero will be with you every step of the way. Therefore, you have the ability to experience happiness everywhere.

You should be happy at school, at home, at your grandparents' house, in the store, at your friend's house, in the library, at baseball practice, in the swimming pool, at your dance recital, and in the car on the way to school. Did I mention school? You should be happy on a vacation, and you should be happy on a field trip. You should be happy at your sister's award ceremony, and you should be happy volunteering at a food pantry.

Happiness doesn't necessarily mean you are having the time of your life. Happiness is simply having positive thoughts. So, as hard as it is to picture, it is possible to be in a dentist's office and experience happiness. If you can figure out how to be happy during a math test, you build superpowers that will get you through things that you haven't even imagined you'll need to face. You'll practice to be ready for disappointments, grief, broken bones, and even calculus. Because you deserve to be happy everywhere, even when—maybe especially when—it's tough. Then you'll be able to spread happiness wherever you go.

WHO should be happy?

Everyone! That's right. I said *everyone* should experience happiness. Your brother, your sister, your mother, your father, your cousins, your neighbors, your teachers, your coaches, your classmates. People you know and people you do not know should be happy. Bullies and the kindest people should be happy. Even cats

should be happy, I think. You get the point. Everyone should be happy.

Wait a minute, who did I forget? Dogs? No, dogs are always happy. YOU—that's right—YOU should be happy.

<u>YOU</u> SHOULD BE HAPPY.

Now that you know the who, what, when, where, and why of happiness, let's move on to one of the most important questions of all: *HOW* can we be happy?

CHAPTER 4

HOW TO BE HAPPY

Let me share a secret. Many people believe that happiness comes and goes. In other words, they believe they have little to no control over when they can be happy. That's because they believe happiness is based on things that they can't really do anything about, like popularity, who gets the best grades, if their parents are cool, and on and on. Sure, these things will make you happy temporarily, but what about the times when you are not popular, or when you do not get the best grades, or when your parents punish you? What then?

Think about a roller coaster. It goes up and down, up and down, a few twists and sharp turns, and up and down some more. Sounds fun, right? Wrong! The roller coaster of life is not fun at all! If you wait for people, things, or events to make you happy, then you will get unlimited rides on the roller coaster of life. When the roller coaster goes up, then you are the happiest kid in your school. Maybe you receive an award or maybe your dad buys you the newest video game—woo-hoo! But when the roller coaster goes down, like if someone makes fun of you or you don't

get invited to a sleepover, then your happiness drops, and you become the most negative kid in your class.

You can never experience true happiness if you are just going along for the ride. The fact is that life will give you ups and downs, twists and turns. Why leave your happiness to chance? Why allow your happiness to depend on your friends or your classmates or your parents? Why should happiness depend on your grades or your accomplishments? Why should happiness depend on how many likes you get on a photo? I am going to teach you how to stop the roller coaster and get off. I prefer you to be on a spaceship instead and head toward the moon!

Without further ado, I will answer the question: HOW?

The only way to be truly happy is to TRAIN YOUR SUPERHERO.

Everyone has a superhero. You were born with one. Yes, little brothers have them too. So do your grandma, your parents, your teachers, and even your best friends. Don't go ask them about it now—they won't know what you are talking about. Your brother will just laugh, and your grandma will ask you to repeat the question. Your parents will say, "Yes, honey, now can you empty the dishwasher?" It is a shame that many people do not know they have a superhero. Imagine if everyone was nice and kind. If everyone helped each other. If all were giving and considerate. Your school would be the best school in the universe. Well, now is the time for everyone to know that they, too, have a superhero.

How much do you know about your mind? What does it look like? How big is it? Where is it? The smartest of humankind have tried to locate the mind for hundreds of years but have not been successful. They only know that the brain has something to do

with the mind. Well, if they would have asked me, then the mystery would have been solved by now. Your mind is located in the superhero world.

In the superhero world, we think of your mind as a city, what we call a Mind Metropolis. Each human has one Mind Metropolis, and every Mind Metropolis belongs to one human. Like people, each city is unique. Even twins get their own Mind Metropolises. So you have a city, your mom has a city, your baby sister has a city. Everyone has a city unlike any other.

Within every city in the mind are citizens. These citizens are what you would call your "thoughts." Citizens are very important. You have between fifty thousand and seventy thousand citizens in your Mind Metropolis each day. Have you ever wondered why your thoughts sound like someone is speaking to you? Superheroes know that your thoughts are actually the voices of the citizens in your Mind Metropolis. The citizens can either improve your city or damage it. They can come and go. Some stay permanently. Others are only visiting.

So why is all of this important to you? Our worlds are deeply connected. The superhero world influences your human world. Whatever happens in your Mind Metropolis directly affects how you act and feel in your real world. And how you act and feel in your world directly affects the condition of the city in your mind.

There are good citizens and there are bad citizens in your Mind Metropolis. You might have heard that your thoughts can be good or bad. Well, that is an understatement. Your thoughts, which we superheroes call your "citizens," have an enormous amount of influence. Good citizens help your city thrive. These citizens only communicate positively. They speak words of love, joy, happiness, gratitude, forgiveness, and other good things. When the good citizens in the city in your mind speak up and are heard, you have the urge to help someone in need, or give a compliment to a stranger, or share something of yours with your sibling.

When the words of the good citizens affect your behavior, your Mind Metropolis grows. Let's say, for instance, you and your best friend got into a big fight over something silly. Your good citizens would speak words of forgiveness and love. They may say, "He didn't really mean what he said. He did not try to hurt your feelings. He was only sad because his parents grounded him. He didn't mean to take it out on you. You should talk to him. Your friendship is more important than a petty argument." If you listened and talked to your friend, your city would immediately start repairs and eventually it would be even better than before.

What about bad citizens? Bad citizens only speak negative words. They speak hate, jealousy, selfishness, revenge, anger, and other things that drag you down. When you hear bad citizens, you have the urge to fight with a friend, argue with your parents, or spread rumors about a classmate. Bad citizens are responsible for damaging your Mind Metropolis, which prevents it from growing. Bad citizens are like vandalizers. When they speak words of hate (in the city in your mind) and your action (in the human world) follows, then your Mind Metropolis stops growing. The negative actions in the human world damage your city in the superhero world. Then repairs need to be made before any growth can occur.

Let's look at an example. Say you were mean to your little brother when he was bothering you. The bad citizens probably said bad things about him. Then you probably said those mean things out loud to your brother. Whenever you are mean to someone else, you cause damage to your own city by listening to bad citizens. That is how bad citizens are directly responsible for you being unhappy.

Citizens are always influencing your behavior; they can cause you to be kind and friendly, but they can also cause you to be mean and rude. These citizens can even cause you to make bad choices like cheating on a test or taking something that isn't yours. This happens when a bunch of bad citizens move into your city with no one to kick them out.

Think about a time when you lashed out at your brother. Do you think you came up with those mean words on your own? No, your city was unprotected, that's all.

If your Mind Metropolis is mostly filled with bad citizens and all you hear is negative voices, then you will be unhappy. Do you remember the definition of happiness? "It is the state of receiving or creating positive thoughts." In other words, happiness occurs whenever your city is full of good citizens.

So if you want to experience happiness, then you need to have good citizens in the city in your mind. Seems easy enough, right?

But there is still one problem: There are no police officers in your Mind Metropolis. There are no firefighters, no doctors or nurses. There is no military. There are no groups that can help your city in a time of need or when your city is in chaos. So how can your city keep good citizens in and kick bad citizens out without the help of those groups? Who can protect your city?

CHAPTER 5

MEET YOUR SUPERHERO

I think you are ready to meet your superhero.

In your world, you are probably just a regular kid. I am sure you can't fly and you don't have the strength to pick up a car with one hand. You don't have X-ray vision or the ability to change forms to blend in with your surroundings either.

Well, you are in luck because you already have a real superhero inside you! In your city (your Mind Metropolis) there are no limits for your superhero, who is always on your side. In the superhero realm, your superhero can fly. Your superhero can pick up a car with one hand. Your superhero doesn't need to change in a telephone booth or gear up in a secret lair, and you don't need a special telephone or signal to bring your superhero to your aid. All you have to do is close your eyes.

Every time you close your eyes, your superhero will appear. When your eyes are closed, you are looking into your Mind Metropolis.

That superhero is the one who will protect the good citizens and kick out the bad ones. Your superhero will defend your Mind

Metropolis against attacks. What is your superhero's name? You get to discover them, so it's up to you.

You might be wondering: Who would attack your Mind Metropolis? Think about how superhero stories work: There's a city. There are good, law-abiding citizens. There's a superhero. But there has to be a bad guy too! Each Mind Metropolis has a superhero, but each also has a villain. The city in your mind needs protection against villains.

Before you run to tell your dad that your sister is a villain, let me explain a little more about the battles in our world. First: your sister is not a villain. In our world, villains are the real enemy. Your nice Mind Metropolis doesn't make citizens bad; all the bad citizens have been sent there by villains. Villains attack different parts of your city by sending bad citizens. Some villains attack the Kindness District. Some attack Belief Boulevard. Others send armies to Honesty Neighborhood. Each villain has an army of bad citizens that will try to damage your Mind Metropolis.

Although villains will try to attack different areas of your city, all villains share one common goal: villains want to prevent you from being who you were created to be. Villains are masterminds who know that you are special, but they do not want *you* to know that. Instead they want you to try to fit in with the crowd. They want you to do what everyone else is doing. They want you to gossip about the kids you do not like. They want you to use bad words. They want you to yell about your brother and sister. They want you to talk back to your parents. They want you to do all the bad things other kids are doing. Villains want you to feel isolated when you are different. In fact, they even want you to feel bad when you are doing what is right.

Villains understand how the condition of your city inside the superhero world will control your actions in the outside world. They want to destroy your world and ours together. If they can constantly send bad citizens to your city, then you will be unhappy, and when you are unhappy your actions will eventually impact the real people around you in a negative way. Villains love this!

This is why it is so important to protect your Mind Metropolis. A city left unprotected is the reason behind every bully in every school. Kids aren't born as bullies; even kids who bully are special and unique, and they want to be happy. They just haven't realized it yet. Their cities have been left unprotected. Their villains are winning.

You cannot allow the villains to win. Your friends cannot allow their villains to win. That is why training your superhero is the key to happiness. A well-trained superhero is the only way to keep good citizens in your city and bad citizens out.

Oh no! I see a villain near your Mind Metropolis! There's no more time to waste. Let the training begin!

CHAPTER 6

TRAINING #1: PAYING ATTENTION

Before your superhero learns how to do the cool stuff, like run faster than the speed of light, your superhero must first learn how to pay attention to the citizens who are in your Mind Metropolis. We know now that citizens are always talking and that you can hear them. But the reason it is important to pay attention to what they say is that citizens influence your actions.

Think about it. You have tons of citizens talking, but sometimes it is difficult to know for sure which one is influencing your actions the most. If you're not paying attention, you could be tricked. For example, have you ever been so annoyed that you snapped at your parents for no reason at all? When they asked you what was wrong, you had to think about why you were annoyed in the first place. That confusion is a clear sign that you were not paying attention to the citizens in your city.

Since citizens in your city directly affect your happiness, it is very important that you pay attention to every citizen so your superhero can pay attention too. Citizens in the superhero realm are very powerful. Some will lead you to laughter. Some will cause you to cry. Some will help you feel inspired, and others will make you feel like a failure.

Think about the last time you were sad. What happened that made you sad? Now think about the citizens who were speaking during that time. Those were the thoughts that made you feel sad. Did your superhero come to the rescue and kick those bad citizens out? Since your superhero has not yet been trained, those destructive citizens were likely allowed to live in your city for quite some time. In fact, some of them may still remain. But what if your superhero was trained to remove these unwelcome citizens?

It's your superhero's job to know each and every citizen who comes into your city. Which ones just moved in. Which ones are visiting. Which are the most influential. Which are suspicious. With so many citizens coming through daily, your superhero must be on guard. Remember, you will probably have tens of thousands of thoughts per day. That is a lot of citizens coming in and out of your city! Your superhero must train in paying attention in order to manage who comes in and who gets to stay.

The more your superhero knows about each citizen, the more prepared and ready your superhero will be when villains attack.

This skill has a simple name and requires one concentrated action. It is called PAYING ATTENTION.

PAYING ATTENTION

GOALS:

☐ Pause throughout the day to discover which thoughts are causing your feelings.

☐ Write down your thoughts after school and before bed.

Pay attention to your thoughts to help your super-hero pay attention to all the citizens. Be aware that the citizens in the city—the thoughts in your mind—are influencing your actions throughout the day. They can change the way you treat your family, your friends, your classmates, even strang-ers. Imagine if someone were whispering in your ear constantly for a week that it is impossible to make the cheerleading squad. Do you think you would be more likely or less likely to try out?

In order to get a grasp on how to manage these citizens, you have to train your superhero by paying attention. The next time you are happy, recognize the thought that made you smile. That's a citizen you want to feel welcome. Also notice when you are unhappy. Which thoughts contributed to your unhappiness? Those citizens need to leave! Make a habit of recognizing the thoughts that cause you to feel a certain way.

But how do you pay attention? It's quite simple, actually. All you have to do is pause. When you are feeling happy or unhappy, stop what you are doing and try to discover the thoughts that are causing you to feel that way. This lets your superhero meet the citizens. Do this multiple times throughout the day until you become used to it.

Try to pay attention all day. Be intentional about noticing all of your happy thoughts and all of your unhappy ones. Then twice a day, spend about ten minutes writing down your thoughts, once after school and again before you go to bed. By doing this, you will be able to capture your thoughts from the two most influential places in your life: school and home.

This exercise is similar to taking notes in class. It is impossible to remember everything that is taught in class. Similarly, it is impossible to remember every thought that occurs throughout the day. That is why it is important to write down your thoughts. Writing them down is the easiest way to detect certain behaviors, since most of your actions begin with thoughts in your mind— the citizens up to no good or citizens doing good deeds in your superhero's city. You have to help your superhero keep track of all those citizens, good and bad.

DOC'S EXAMPLE #1

THINKING ABOUT A FRIEND

Emma is one of Dr. RJ's patients. She always came to her appointments with the biggest smile on her face. Emma even smiled when she sneezed.

One day, when Emma arrived for her appointment, Dr. RJ and I immediately knew that something was wrong because she wasn't smiling.

"What's wrong?" Dr. RJ asked.

"Nothing really," Emma replied.

"You have a smile that can be recognized from miles away, but I don't see it today," Dr. RJ said. We could tell by Emma's short answers and the expression on her face that she was not experiencing happiness. So we began to teach Emma the first step of training her superhero: paying attention to her thoughts.

Emma confessed that she has been sad lately. It had to do with her best friend Amanda. She couldn't figure out why she and Amanda were not close anymore. She kept having thoughts that Amanda was not a good friend.

"What changed?" Dr. RJ asked. But Emma could not put her finger on when the change occurred.

Dr. RJ suggested Emma start writing down her thoughts twice a day, once after school and once before bed. (I knew this was to help her superhero.) When she did this for a few days, she realized when the tension between herself and Amanda began: Three weeks ago, Emma saw Amanda hanging out with other classmates without her. Emma didn't want to seem jealous, so she never asked Amanda about what she saw. Although there was no reason to be upset with Amanda, Emma realized that seeing Amanda having fun with other friends made her feel that Amanda preferred those other friends over her.

Emma discovered this truth because she found it written in her journal every day. Every time she wrote down her thoughts, "Amanda laughing with new friends because she likes them better than me" was on her list. Aha! That was the bad citizen!

Emma discovered the cause of her tension and immediately called Amanda to apologize. Amanda was not trying to replace Emma as her friend after all. Emma's superhero banished all the citizens who had been trying to spread bad feelings about their friendship. Emma had an appointment two weeks later, and guess who had her smile back—Emma.

GOALS:

☑ Pause throughout the day to discover which thoughts are causing your feelings.

☑ Write down your thoughts after school and before bed.

CHAPTER 7

TRAINING #2:
KNOW YOUR ENEMY

Now that your superhero has mastered the skill of paying attention, it's time to learn the next important skill. Your superhero must learn how to identify the grand evil plans of the villains.

In sports, the better you understand the strategy of the other team, the better your chances are of winning. It's similar in the superhero realm. The better we understand how villains attack, the better our chances of defeating them. Before I teach you about the attack strategies villains use, we must first understand every villain's main goal.

The number-one goal of all villains is to send bad citizens to your Mind Metropolis so that you will be unhappy. Bad citizens are crude, rude, and have major attitude. These are the citizens you do not want. When they are in your city, they only speak negative words. Since you hear them, bad citizens can cause you to say things that you do not really want to say and do things that you really don't want to do.

Have you ever given in to peer pressure? Maybe your friends dared you to do something dangerous like ride your scooter as fast as you could down a big hill. It wasn't really your friends' words that convinced you to do it; it was the bad citizens in your city who convinced you to make the wrong choice. A villain sent them with a mission to create unhappiness. The bad citizens are the ones who repeated over and over to "just do it." Without a trained superhero, you might function like a robot, repeating everything you hear and doing everything they command.

Bad citizens are also the ones who tell you to lie to your parents. They tell you to leave a mean comment on someone's post. They tell you to retaliate when someone does something mean to you and to hold grudges with classmates. Every time you have said something hurtful or anytime you did something out of anger, it came from the bad citizens in your city.

You see, villains understand that if the city in your mind is run by bad citizens, then you will be unhappy. The more time you spend unhappy, the less you will be able to impact your real world in a positive way. Your unhappiness will cause you to forget that you are unique and special and that only you can impact your world in your own special way.

Can you see the importance of training your superhero? Without a trained superhero, you will experience the roller-coaster effect, up and down, up and down. One day you will feel good and have happy moments. The next day you will be angry and upset. I see it all the time. Kids allow their circumstances to decide how they should feel. If everything goes their way, and everyone does what they want them to do, and all they hear is the word "yes," then they feel great. They think they are happy. But if something doesn't go as planned, or someone disagrees, or no one is paying attention to them, then they feel down. They are unhappy. All of this occurs because their villains have taken over their cities with armies of bad citizens.

Now that we understand the goal of villains, let's look at how they attack. They do so by sending three main types of bad citizens. Eventually, we'll learn to protect against them. But for now, let's look at the different types so your superhero will be able to recognize them.

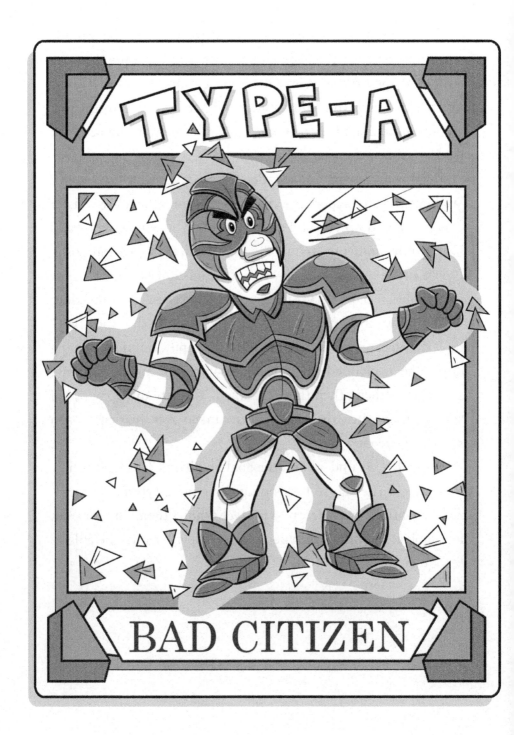

TYPE-A
DESTRUCTION STYLE: fast and loud

The first type of bad citizen is Type-A. These are the most common bad citizens. They are loud and they are fast. Villains have an entire army of loud and fast bad citizens. They are extremely effective. Since you hear the voices of all the citizens in your city, you are more likely to hear loud citizens over quiet ones. It is no different than in your school cafeteria. You do not hear the quiet conversations, but often you can hear the table next to you if the kids are talking loudly. If the bad citizens are so loud that you cannot hear the good citizens, then you will likely follow their directions—you will say what they tell you to say or do what they tell you to do. This happens in the blink of an eye. They are so fast it is difficult to see them coming.

Villains usually send Type-A bad citizens randomly, like when you're sitting in science class and think, "My teacher's voice is annoying" or "The girl next to me is wearing an ugly dress."

Villains can also send these citizens as a reaction right after an event happens in your world. In fact, they are usually the first on the scene. Let's say one of your classmates tripped and fell down at lunch. Type-A bad citizens are the ones who told you to laugh loud so all of your friends could hear. Or when you were in an argument with your sibling, Type-A bad citizens told you the most hurtful thing to say. Or when your parents told you to do something, these bad citizens were the ones who told you to respond in a disrespectful manner.

Sometimes your city is attacked so much that it can cause you to think obsessively about that one thing. For instance, do you know anyone who is addicted to video games? All they can do is think about video games. When they are playing, nothing can interrupt them. Their parents give them an hour a day of video-game time. What happens when their hour is up? It doesn't end well. The bad citizens who encourage them to play and obsess over video games are still in their city.

The person might ignore their parents when their time is up. Or they may get upset and start an argument in order to try and get what the bad citizens tell them they need.

If you're not careful, these bad citizens can move into your city permanently. They will speak the same message so much it will become part of your personality. As you can see, these Type-A citizens are very effective at their job.

TYPE-B
DESTRUCTION STYLE: slow, quiet, and sneaky

The second type of bad citizen is Type-B. Unlike the Type-As, they move in slowly so as not to be detected. They purposefully do not draw a lot of attention. In fact, Type-B citizens are so quiet it will take time before you believe what they are telling you.

While Type-A citizens want you to function like a robot, Type-Bs try to trick you. They want you to believe something that is not true, and they spread lies over time until you believe them. That is why they must sneak into your city without making noise—because convincing takes time.

Type-Bs use opinions to their advantage by treating opinions as facts. This is so damaging to your Mind Metropolis because opinions cannot be proven. Therefore, unless your superhero stops them, Type-B citizens help villains by making you believe something that is not true.

For example, Type-B citizens will tell you that your younger brother is the most annoying brother in the world, maybe in the universe. Since there is no actual standard measurement of annoyance, that statement is an opinion. If you accept it as a fact, though, you will treat your younger brother unkindly. You'll be mean not just when you fight, but all the time. However, if your superhero does the job right, those whispers will be silenced, and you'll learn to expect and accept your little brother's behavior; he's just doing what little brothers do.

Let's look at another example. Say your parents grounded you. Type-B citizens would tell you things like, "You have the meanest parents in the world," "Your parents like your sister more than you," and "They would never ground your sister for the same mistake." Do you see how the Type-B citizens try to get you to focus on opinions instead of facts? The fact is you are grounded. Everything else is just an opinion. If Type-B citizens can get you to focus on the opinions, then you are unhappy and you may even begin to resent your parents, and the villain does a victory dance.

Type-B citizens like to get you to focus on negative opinions about other people, but what they love even more is if they can get you to focus on negative opinions about yourself. They absolutely love to tell you what you can't do and why you are not special. They love to get you to believe negative "I am" statements: "I am not pretty enough." "I am not smart enough." "I am not good enough." "I am not loved." Can you imagine just how damaging these lies are?

Type-B citizens know that if they were loud, your superhero would find them and kick them out. So they are very quiet. They whisper these lies to you over time until you start to believe them. They are so tricky you may not even know they've convinced you.

In some cases, the only way to determine if you believe their lies is to look at your actions and ask, "Why?" Why didn't you raise your hand in class when you knew the answer? Why didn't you try out for the soccer team? Why didn't you sit next to the classmate you wanted to talk to at lunch?

If you take the time to answer the "why" question, then you will know what lies you have been listening to. You will be able to determine what negative opinions you have accepted as facts. Type-B bad citizens want you to sulk and give up because while you are sulking, you are unable to impact your world in your own special way.

TYPE-C
DESTRUCTION STYLE: follows natural disasters

The last type of bad citizen is Type-C. These bad citizens are very dangerous.

Type-Cs can be fast or slow. They can be loud or quiet. What makes these bad citizens so dangerous is that they occur only after a certain type of event: after a natural disaster in your Mind Metropolis. Natural disasters, in the superhero realms, are negative events that happen in your human world that are out of your

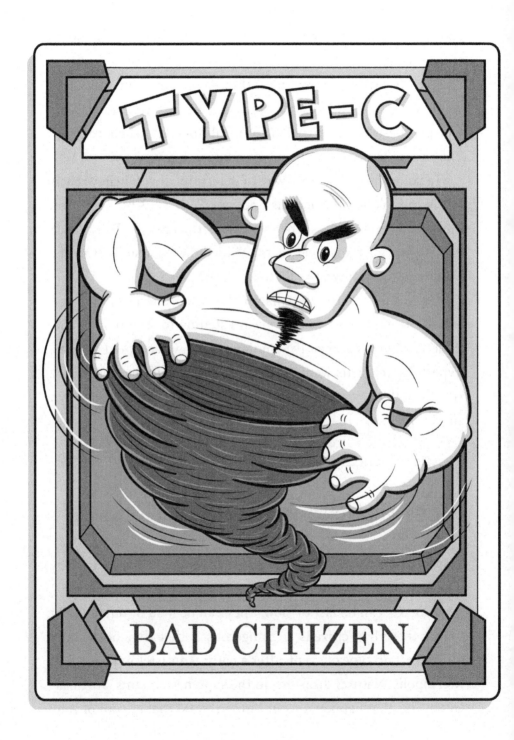

control. Bad things can happen to good people. It is unfortunate, but it happens all the time.

Type-C bad citizens come when something bad happens that is completely out of your control. For example, if your parents got a divorce, you may have felt your life spinning around you. In the superhero realm, a tornado hit your Mind Metropolis. Getting bullied could cause a shake-up of what you thought you knew about yourself. In our world, an earthquake occurred in your city. Breaking your leg caused a rush of loss that you wouldn't be able to play soccer for the rest of the season. In the superhero realm, a tsunami hit your Mind Metropolis. When a natural disaster occurs, you feel out of control. Natural disasters occur in every human's Mind Metropolis, and they cannot be avoided. So where do the villains come in?

Villains know that natural disasters cause chaos naturally, so your Mind Metropolis is the most vulnerable during this time. During so much chaos, villains send in Type-C bad citizens. These Type-Cs will tell you that whatever you are experiencing now will be much worse tomorrow and the next day and the next day and so on. They know that humans almost always look into the future when they experience a devastating or tragic event. If they can get you to see an unhappy future, then they have won.

Type-C bad citizens use devastating events to their advantage. They know that it's natural for you to be unhappy when something bad happens. If you could focus on each moment as it happens by thinking about the present instead of fearing the future, then your unhappiness would fade. But if Type-C bad citizens can get you to focus on a bad future, then your unhappiness will grow.

Type-C bad citizens want you to focus on a bad future that might never happen. They want you to be unhappy about tomorrow. Although no one in your world or mine can predict what will happen tomorrow, these citizens try to predict it for you, and they try to make you scared. These citizens are a danger to your city because it is difficult to experience happiness when you are not looking forward to tomorrow.

Now that you know about the types of bad citizens, we must train your superhero to identify the three types of bad citizens. Recognizing the different types of bad citizens is very important. It will help your superhero decide how to fight when defending your city.

For example, at a sleepover, a villain might prevent you from experiencing happiness by drawing your attention to how your best friend is spending more time with another friend. Those are Type-B citizens trying to convince you that your friend likes another friend more than you.

What if a classmate posted an embarrassing photo of you on social media? Your villain will send in Type-C bad citizens trying to tell you what is going to happen in the future. They will say that the entire class will laugh at you in school, and then the photo will go viral and the entire world will eventually see it and make fun of you. (Type-Cs love to exaggerate.)

The better your superhero is at identifying the different types of bad citizens, the more prepared your superhero will be against any attack.

SUPERHERO WORKOUT #2
KNOW YOUR ENEMY

GOALS:

☐ Understand the strategies and the ultimate goal of the enemy

☐ Identify the three types of negative thoughts

Since you are writing down your thoughts each day, you are ready to take your workout to the next level. Each day, identify all of the thoughts that are negative. Circle all thoughts that made you sad, angry, upset, agitated, annoyed, depressed, or unhappy. Then try to figure out which thoughts came from Type-A, Type-B, or Type-C bad citizens.

Write "Type-A" next to any thoughts, whether random or associated with some event, that encouraged a negative action or led you to say something negative.

Write "Type-B" next to thoughts that got you to focus on the negative opinions about a person—including yourself.

Write "Type-C" next to any negative thoughts about the future that came after a negative event happened to you that was out of your control.

Some events may cause thoughts from all three categories. Let's say, for instance, you just discovered that your crush likes your best friend. Type-A thoughts may convince you to start a rumor about your crush or to treat your best friend differently. Type-B thoughts may cause you to question your looks or personality. Type-C thoughts may cause extreme sadness as you envision the rest of the school year alone.

DOC'S EXAMPLE #2
A DISASTROUS MOVE

Summer vacation was one week away, which meant Dr. RJ's office was usually full of laughs and smiles. When Chris came to the office in tears, Dr. RJ immediately rushed to talk with him. He discovered Chris and his family were moving as soon as school was over. Chris was very upset with his dad since he was the one to make the decision.

"I don't want to move, and he can't make me!" shouted Chris. "What about my friends and my teammates? What about school?" Chris loved his school.

Dr. RJ talked to Chris about disappointment and sadness. Dr. RJ had to switch schools when he was Chris's age. He taught Chris about how thoughts can cause negative feelings about the future and how those negative feelings will affect his actions. He encouraged Chris to focus on paying attention to his feelings and figuring out what kinds of thoughts were affecting him so his superhero could recognize the bad citizens. Dr. RJ and Chris said their goodbyes since Chris and his family would be moving soon.

Weeks later, Dr. RJ was excited to receive an email from Chris's mom. She thanked Dr. RJ for giving Chris a copy of *How to Train Your Superhero*. She said that Chris was so much happier now. Chris realized that his thoughts were causing his anger and disappointment. In fact, he was able to notice how the villain used Type-C citizens to convince him that the move would be the worst mistake in his life. When he recognized the power of identifying his citizens, his superhero was able to shut down the bad citizens and defeat his villain.

Chris realized that the thoughts that caused his anger and disappointment were not from himself but were sent to him by a villain. Once he realized they were against his happiness, he no longer listened to those thoughts. His superhero was able to kick out the Type-C bad citizens and let Chris move on with his life. Even though Chris missed his friends, his teammates, and his school, he did not allow disappointment to stand in the way of his happiness. He made an effort to enjoy the move and to meet new friends. Chris even apologized to his dad for blaming him. He told his dad to not take it personally since it wasn't Chris, it was his villain who caused him to act out. Dad was just happy to see Chris smile again.

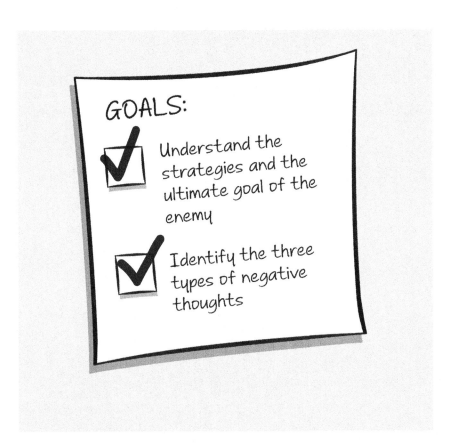

CHAPTER 8

TRAINING #3:
A QUICK OFFENSE IS
A STRONG DEFENSE

Now it's time for the part that you have been waiting for: How to kick butt. How to defeat the villains and kick out bad citizens.

Just like villains have a game plan for attack, we superheroes have a game plan too. We have one goal and one goal only: keep bad citizens out of your Mind Metropolis. Over the next chapters, I will teach you three main strategies for achieving this goal.

The first is the quick attack. It is the easiest and fastest mode of attack. Your superhero will use it anytime they see a bad citizen. It will be your first line of defense. No matter which type of bad citizen, if the citizens are bad, your superhero will kick them out. This attack is very effective against Type-A bad citizens because, remember, they are fast—your superhero can be just as fast kicking them out. If Type-A citizens enter your city and tell you to say something mean to a stranger or make fun

of a classmate, kick them out. If citizens enter your city and tell you to argue with your teacher or to ignore your parents, kick them out. If citizens enter your city to distract you from focusing in class or studying for a test, kick them out.

If Type-B citizens tell you that no one likes your freckles, your superhero should kick them out. If Type-B citizens tell you that you are too overweight to be a cheerleader or too short to play basketball, kick them out.

If Type-C citizens tell you that no one will want to be your friend after you told the teacher about the students who were cheating, have your superhero kick them out. Your superhero should try the quick defense for any type of bad citizen.

Let's say that you and a classmate were talking and another classmate rudely interrupted your conversation, as if you were invisible. Type-A bad citizens would immediately rush into your Mind Metropolis screaming at you to say something rude to your classmate. If your superhero doesn't kick those bad citizens out quickly, chances are you would say something that you would regret.

Remember, the longer these citizens stay, the harder it will be to defeat your villain. That is why swift action—a quick counter-attack—to kick them out is necessary.

SUPERHERO WORKOUT #3

KAPOW!

GOALS:

☐ Get rid of negative thoughts before you speak or act

☐ Apologize for any negative words or actions

Every time a negative thought enters your mind, help your superhero quickly get rid of the thought. Choose a one- or two-syllable word or phrase such as "Go," "Pow," "Leave," or "Get out." Find something you can say out loud or under your breath, or just in your mind if you must. This word will help remind you that negative thoughts cannot stay in your mind. When you say the power word, your superhero will be able to quickly kick out a bad citizen. The longer the bad citizens stay in your mind, the more harm they can cause. As soon as you recognize you are thinking about saying something or doing something negative, immediately say the word of your choice and try to imagine your superhero kicking that bad citizen out!

What happens if you do not kick the thoughts out of your mind in time and you do or say something negative? At this point, say your word of choice to eliminate the thought—it is not too late for your superhero to kick out a citizen. And then apologize to anyone you have wronged. Ask for forgiveness. Apologizing doesn't mean that you will never do something or say something mean ever again in your life. Apologizing means that you recognize your mistake, you feel bad about making the mistake, and you will *try* not to make the same mistake again.

What if you *do* make the mistake again? Apologize again. Apologizing takes courage and it builds character. When you take the time to acknowledge how your mistake affected someone else, it shows how mature you are. What if the other person hurt you too? You still want to apologize first. Superheroes cannot force another superhero to do anything, but superheroes can lead by example. If the other person's superhero is trained, then I am sure that person will apologize also. But remember, apologies should be given freely without any expectation of an apology in return.

At this point you have mastered recognizing your thoughts since you are writing them down each day. You have also learned how to identify the different types of negative thoughts in your mind. Now that you have a power word, you are ready to really give your superhero a workout.

MAKE A LIST: List citizens you've encountered during the day. (If you just did Superhero Workout #2, you can use that list!) Write a check mark next to any thought you recognized as a Type-A bad citizen that your superhero kicked out of your Mind Metropolis in time; the check mark is for the bad citizens you banished before you did or said something negative. Also write a check mark next to the thoughts where you apologized— yes, you still get a check mark even though your superhero didn't kick the bad citizen out in time, because you still did the right thing.

Write an X mark next to any thoughts where your superhero did not kick the bad citizen out before it made you do something wrong and you haven't apologized for the mistake. Try your best to apologize to any person who was affected by your mistake.

DOC'S EXAMPLE #3
BANISHING BAD CITIZENS

Esther came into the office excited because Dr. RJ was going to remove her expander. With two pops and less than a minute later, the expander was out.

"I can say 'A skunk sat on a stump and thunk the stump stunk, but the stump thunk the skunk stunk' without spitting on my friends."

Dr. RJ and Esther's parents laughed.

"Guess what?" said Esther. "My superhero won yesterday."

"How so?" asked Dr. RJ.

"My friend Bailey really dislikes this girl in our class. Yesterday, Bailey told me something very mean about her. I was tempted to tell all of my classmates. I kept having thoughts telling me to share what Bailey told me. At lunch I was sitting with my friends and I just said, 'NO!'—my super-hero's power word.

"I immediately went back to Bailey and told her that she shouldn't tell anyone else what she told me. Our classmate did not deserve to be treated like that. Rumors can really hurt, and they're usually not even true. I told Bailey she shouldn't spread rumors even if she disliked someone. I was shocked that Bailey agreed. Then I actually took it a step further and started being nice to our classmate. I told Bailey that I would start being kind because I want our class to be friendlier. I asked Bailey if that would be okay because I do value our friendship, and Bailey said it was."

What Esther did was show her whole class that her superhero is protecting her Mind Metropolis. Not only did Esther stop a potentially devastating experience for her classmate, she also stood up to her friend Bailey in a gentle and loving way. Esther asked Bailey for permission to be nice to their classmate to show that Esther truly valued their friendship. (If Esther had started being nice without mentioning it to Bailey, that could have possibly sent the wrong message to Bailey.) This is a perfect example of leading by example. Esther and her superhero are so strong! If you are in a similar situation, like maybe your friends are being mean to other kids, you have an opportunity to help everyone be better. You can explain how they can feel happier without causing pain to others.

CHAPTER 9

TRAINING #4:
SUPERPOWER

This is where the real fun begins. Every superhero has a superpower. Although your superhero will easily defeat most bad citizens with quick attacks, some bad citizens are harder to kick out of your city, like Type-B and Type-C citizens. These are the ones on which your superhero must really use superpowers. In order to use superpowers, we must have enough energy built up. Every time we use our superpowers, it drains our superhero energy, so keep that in mind. It is easier to kick out all types of bad citizens as soon as they come to the city instead of waiting and having to use our superpowers.

All superpowers produce the same overall result: they transform bad citizens into good citizens. A superpower is the most powerful tool your superhero has to defeat your villain. A superpower is your superhero's second line of defense. If you were unable to kick out Type-B and Type-C bad citizens with a quick attack, then it is time to use a superpower. Bad citizens often

sneak into your Mind Metropolis and damage it from the inside. A superpower will not only let your superhero stop damage to your city but will actually use these bad citizens to help repair things by turning them into good citizens.

Before you begin training your superhero to use a superpower, you must first pick a specific superpower. Pick whatever you want. Give your superhero the coolest superpower you can think of. Kicking out bad citizens is helpful, but sometimes it's even better for superheroes to capture the Type-B citizens and turn them around. Since Type-B bad citizens are so sneaky, they'll often find their way back to your city if they don't change their ways. Your superhero's power will capture them so they can be transformed from a bad citizen to a good citizen.

Believe it or not, visualizing the superpower will motivate you whenever it is time for your superhero to step up. Superheroes do not brag, but I must admit, my superpower is pretty cool. I have the ability to straighten anything that is crooked or out of alignment. I'm sure you have never heard of a superpower like that before. My city is always intact. After intense battles with villains, my city is usually a wreck. With my superpower, I am able to bring buildings back to their original form. I can do the same with vehicles and roads too. This superpower allows me to capture bad citizens because when my city is orderly, I can find them more quickly. Then I straighten out their crooked intentions and show them how great things are when the city runs smoothly, so they're helpful instead of harmful.

One of my allies is invisible. She can catch many bad citizens and turn them into good citizens because they never see her coming. Her city is one of the safest since it's nearly impossible for villains to defeat her.

I've seen superheroes with lightning bolts that shoot from their chest. I've seen some who can fly faster than the speed of sound. Some have extreme strength, infrared vision, or the ability to control metal. Whichever superpower your superhero has, all superpowers achieve the same thing: they turn bad citizens into good citizens. Superheroes like to kick out most bad citizens because it is much easier to kick them out than capture them. But there are some bad citizens who require superpowers. Some citizens are great at sneaking back into your city so your superhero has to kick out the same bad citizens over and over again. If they can turn that bad citizen into a good citizen, then villains may think twice about attacking your city. Not only is your superhero getting rid of a bad citizen, your city is gaining a good citizen.

Before you start training with your hero's superpower, you must understand the time commitment this will take. Taking a bad citizen and turning them into a good one is very difficult. The only way for superheroes to master superpowers is to practice, practice—and practice some more. This practice will give you both the confidence and the techniques needed when the time comes for superpowers in battle.

Some thoughts are not easily expelled from your mind. Some will stick for hours, days, months, and years. This technique gives your superhero the power to take control of the negative thoughts and change them into positive thoughts. This technique is best used when the thoughts are opinions since these thoughts are not backed by facts.

Remember these bad citizens' words?

"My brother is mom's favorite."
"I'm too short to play basketball."
"No one in my class likes me."
"I am not pretty."

These are all opinions. The problem with believing these opinions is that your actions will reflect that the opinions are true. Why not choose to believe the opposite of the negative opinion? Let your superhero turn those bad citizens into good ones! As you start to believe the opposite of the negative thought, you will notice that your actions will change. If you believe that your mom loves you and your brother the same, then you won't give your brother such a hard time. If you believe that you are good at basketball, you will be motivated to practice harder. If you believe that your classmates like you, then you will make more of an effort to try to get to know them. If you believe that you are beautiful, then you will carry yourself like you are.

A superpower is truly powerful. It can change not only the way you feel about yourself, but also your results. Let's say that you are dreading studying for your math test because you believe you are not good at math. Sure, you do not score As on every test, but that doesn't mean you are not good at math. Being good at something is an opinion. Therefore, why not start believing that you are good at math? Let your superhero get citizens to start saying that you are good at math. Start smiling when you are doing math homework. Tell your friends and family that math is your favorite subject.

Only you can determine if you are good at something. Just because you get a C or F in math does not mean you are not good at it. Grades can only hurt you if you let them. A letter grade is designed to tell you which direction to move toward. If you receive an A, then continue moving in the same direction. If you get an F, then change directions. It is that simple. Don't let the grades define you as someone good at math or someone bad at math.

If you go into a school year hearing the bad citizens who say, "You're not good at math," you'll be less interested in math and more concerned with feeling bad. That means you will not be as motivated to study or learn more about the subject. Your mind will also create fear and anxiety around tests. A lack of confidence means you probably won't do as well—you might second-guess your answers. Not to mention that anxiety clouds your decision-making ability.

If your superhero could switch those citizens so they'd tell you lots of good things about math, you may find the subject more interesting and less stressful. It may cause you to study more and work on your skills rather than dwelling on your mistakes. You'll notice over time that you have what it takes to do well in math. The good citizens can help build confidence that can even help during tests. Once you believe that you are good at math, your actions will follow and your grades will improve.

Now this may seem too good to be true. Can you really become better at a sport by believing you are good at the sport? Can you really improve your grades by changing your beliefs? The answer is *yes*. But do not take my word for it. Let's try target practice. Once you believe in your superhero's superpower, then the sky is the limit.

SUPERHERO WORKOUT #4
TARGET PRACTICE

GOALS:

☐ Complete target practice: identify thoughts that focus on opinions rather than facts

☐ Believe the opposite of the negative thoughts

Choose a food item that you dislike the most. First you will make a commitment that you will eat this item as much as possible until you love it. (Don't even think about trying to use ice cream. You can *kapow* that thought right out of your mind!) Choose a healthy item that you find disgusting—brussels sprouts, tofu, raw kale, broccoli, anything that usually brings on your *yuck* face. The goal is to train your mind into believing that you love this food.

Each day you want to have positive thoughts about the item. Tell yourself that it tastes good every time you chew it. Tell others that you crave it. Tell your parents that you love it and it's your new favorite food to eat. Look at it and say the word "yum." Picture your superhero grabbing the bad citizen who used to say "yuck," and then imagine the bad citizen saying "yum" instead. Do whatever you need to do until the day you truly enjoy eating it and you actually believe it's good.

It may take days, weeks, or even months until your superhero successfully passes this training. This training is so important because it gives you faith that changing a negative opinion about a person (including yourself), place, or thing is possible—it *is* possible to change your actions, and your results, by simply believing. You will understand the power of the mind (and your superhero!). The real superpower is that you are the one who decides what you believe and what you don't.

POWER MOVE: Take your list from Superhero Workout #2. Focus on any thoughts identified as Type-B and begin working toward changing those thoughts into positive ones. Just like with the food, make steps toward believing the opposite until it's true for you. Keep in mind that this may take time. Generally this does not happen overnight. The more you are able to truly believe the opposite of a negative thought, the more powerful your superhero will become and the more you will be able to impact your world in your own special way.

DOC'S EXAMPLE #4
STANDING TALL

Sara was a very happy patient. The summer before high school, she came for an appointment. One of Dr. RJ's assistants complimented her on her height since she had gotten a little taller. Sara immediately broke down and expressed how much she hated her height. He asked her why, and she said it was because someone told her boys didn't like tall girls.

After learning how to train her superhero, Sara realized that her height was perfectly fine. Her superhero got better and better about getting her citizens to be supportive. Sara started to believe, like the rest of us, that her height was perfect for her. She told herself that every day. Being tall helped her be such a great volleyball player, and someday, the right person would appreciate her height. She realized that she should never wish herself to be smaller or lesser in any way. She noticed that many pro athletes and models are tall. She started wearing shoes to make herself look even taller. She wore stripes, which emphasized her height. Sara continued taking actions to show that she was proud of her height until she actually started liking the fact that she was tall.

GOALS:

☑ Complete target practice: identify thoughts that focus on opinions rather than facts

☑ Believe the opposite of the negative thoughts

CHAPTER 10

TRAINING #5:
SIDEKICK

Your superhero has learned to kick out bad citizens quickly, and you have both learned how to use superpowers, but that's still not enough to defeat all the villains. There is one final method of defense.

Imagine that a hurricane came to your Mind Metropolis—there's damage and chaos everywhere. Remember the Type-C bad citizens? How will your superhero contain the natural disaster and the Type-C bad citizens that have flooded your city? A quick counterattack will not be effective since there are too many bad citizens for your superhero to defeat at once. The superpower may not be as effective since superpowers take a while to perfect and cannot transform things that are out of your control. (Unfortunately, your superhero can't turn a hurricane into a bright, sunny day.)

Imagine that there is a rumor going around school that you cheated on a test. You would be devastated because you know that you study hard and you would never cheat. At first, you would have thoughts like, "Why did someone say this about me?" Then, you would start to have negative thoughts about the future such as, "My classmates will never treat me the same. They will always call me a cheater." How would you handle that? You could try to ignore the thoughts (quick attack). You could try to start thinking that your classmates will actually believe that you are one of the smartest kids in school (superpower). But what if your quick attack and your superpower don't work? What's left?

You have to call in reinforcements. You must bring in a sidekick for your superhero. Every superhero needs (and has) a sidekick. In the superhero realm, a sidekick evens the playing field. If the villains are a negative force that prevents you from being who you were created to be, then a sidekick is a positive force that reminds you of who you were created to be. Your sidekick reminds you that you are special and that you have the power to change your world. Your superhero should not fight every battle alone. Sometimes there are just too many bad citizens for your superhero to handle at once! Sometimes your superhero has no energy left to fight. The sidekick will help.

My sidekick's name is SuperTooth, and he's faster than any jet. His cape turns into fire when he uses supersonic speed. It's pretty cool. I'm sorry you won't get to meet him. He is busy watching Doc's city while I train you.

Superheroes need their sidekicks at different times. I only bring SuperTooth along during tough battles or have him substitute for me when I'm doing these teaching gigs. However, every superhero must bring their sidekick when natural disasters hit. We never try to handle the devastation from a natural disaster

alone. Hurricanes, earthquakes, tornadoes . . . they are too tough for any superhero to contain without help. If you sense Type-C bad citizens, bring in the sidekick!

Like perfecting any team, practice is important. Your superhero and sidekick must practice a game plan. How will they defend your city when there are multiple attacks from villains? How will they handle a villain attacking and bad citizens rushing in?

You can take actions to cause your sidekick to join your superhero in battle. Remember, our worlds are deeply connected. What you do in your human world affects our superhero world, and what happens in our world affects your world.

You might bring in your superhero's sidekick if you need to feel better about something that happened to you that was out of your control, if you need something that inspires or motivates you, or if you need help finding a positive outlook on the future.

Sometimes humans are overloaded with negative thoughts and feel stressed or unhappy. Everyone will experience stress from time to time. Stress, if you don't get rid of it, can hurt your mind and body. You must find healthy ways to help yourself.

Do you enjoy hiking or skating? How about listening to music or hanging out with a friend? During times of stress, turn to things that inspire you or that make you feel better. When you do these positive actions in your world, they bring the sidekick to join your superhero in battle. This increases the chances of beating your villains. These activities allow you to escape the situation and "clear your mind" (in our world, we say "kick out bad citizens"). Doing these things can actually help you solve the problem that is stressing you out. Sometimes it takes sharing your problems out loud or clearing your mind to discover a solution. Whenever you choose actions in your human world that relieve stress, then in our world your sidekick will join your superhero to clean up any natural disaster that could devastate your Mind Metropolis.

SUPERHERO WORKOUT #5
CALLING IN A SIDEKICK

GOALS:

☐ Create your list

☐ Turn to your list whenever you are feeling down

Write down a list of the things you love to do—things you are passionate about, things that make you happy, or things that inspire you. Maybe reading, painting, playing video games, playing a sport, talking to your parents, confiding in your friends, listening to music? What about exercise?

Or spending time with animals or in nature? This list is what you will turn to when you are feeling down or unhappy. Writing these activities down will serve as a reminder that you have help—and that you can give your superhero help when they need it.

It can be easy to forget that you have the help necessary to overcome times when you are unhappy. You don't have to wait until life improves or until you get over it. You can cure the unhappiness right away. It is similar to when you have a headache. You can suffer through it until it goes away by itself or you can do something about it like taking medicine or using relaxation techniques.

Sometimes we suffer through unhappiness until it goes away. The problem with doing that is sometimes it doesn't really go away. It just becomes hidden. Then the next time you experience unhappiness, it will build upon your old unhappiness. This will continue until all of a sudden you start overreacting to everything.

You may have seen your friends lash out at their parents over something that was not really a big deal. Or maybe they became extremely angry over something you did that they would usually just laugh about. There was something really bad in their cities, but they pretended it wasn't there until it couldn't be ignored. Don't wait for unhappiness to just go away naturally because often it does not actually disappear on its own; you, your superhero, and that trusty sidekick need to do some work.

To work on your happiness, post your list of positive actions where you can see it. Maybe put it up on your wall. Put it in your bathroom on the mirror. Put it in your phone. You want to be reminded that you have help. If you want extra credit for this homework, try adding to your list the proven methods to help with stress such as exercising, meditation, rest, and disconnecting from technology. These things will help you overcome negative thoughts—they will call over that sidekick.

Whether you are stressed, sad, or angry, turn to this list for help. When Doc is stressed, he exercises, listens to Christian music, and prays. And there is one other thing he does, but you must first promise to not tell anyone: he eats ice cream and cookies. (Shhh . . . he will treat me like a bad citizen if he finds out I told you.) But all those things are like a beacon to tell SuperTooth to come help me, and SuperTooth always comes through.

DOC'S EXAMPLE #5
HELP IS ON THE WAY

Bryan was one of Dr. RJ's patients who stood out the most. He was never happy at his appointments. He would not speak to anyone. He didn't smile. Dr. RJ couldn't even get him to open up—Bryan would not share how he felt. At one appointment, Dr. RJ pulled Bryan's mom to the side to ask if everything was okay. Bryan's mom mentioned that she could not figure out what was going on with her son either. She said that Bryan was bullied in the fifth grade, so they changed schools. Bryan's mom had checked with the principal and teachers to make sure Bryan was not getting bullied at the new school. They assured her that he was not.

Dr. RJ gave Bryan's mom a copy of *How to Train Your Superhero*. Bryan eventually shared with his mom that he felt depressed. He could not understand why he had been bullied, and he was afraid that it might happen again at his new school. Bryan's mom helped find a counselor who would help with his depression.

Once Bryan trained his superhero, he understood the importance of asking for help. He realized that there are some battles we can't face alone. Over the course of a year, Dr. RJ and his staff watched Bryan transition into a more confident and happier patient. Bryan shared that he often turned to his list when he was feeling down. Bryan's favorite activities are baseball and swimming. He said that he feels free from any worries when he plays baseball. His superhero gets the help they need to do a great job keeping his city protected.

GOALS:

- ✓ Create your list

- ✓ Turn to your list whenever you are feeling down

Sometimes we experience devastating circumstances or difficult situations. Many times these events in our life are out of our control. They come unexpectedly and they can be quite overwhelming. We are not designed to deal with these circumstances alone. We must ask for help.

If you are suffering from depression, feeling over-whelmed, or having thoughts of suicide, it is important that you share that with your loved ones so that they can get you the help you need. It is okay to ask for help. No matter how big or how small the matter is, do not try to get through it alone. Ask for help.

National Suicide Prevention Lifeline:
1-800-273-8255

CHAPTER 11

TRAINING #6: THE POWER OF HAPPINESS

This is the final stage of your training. You and your superhero have learned how to defend your Mind Metropolis against the attacks of the villains. You have learned how to kick bad citizens out of your city, how to turn bad citizens into good citizens, and how your superhero, with the help of a sidekick, can overcome any damage from bad citizens and natural disasters. The final step of training is learning how to attract good citizens.

Until now, your superhero has focused on defense. A strong defense is important and will help you experience happiness. Although a good defense is necessary, your happiness will be limited without a quick offense. When you watch sports, offense is what attracts most spectators. In basketball, dunks or three-point shots are more exciting than blocks or steals. In football, a touchdown is more exciting than a sack. In baseball, a home run

is more exciting than a strike. It is the same in our world. Defense is important, but offense is exciting. Your city will not develop without good citizens. The more good citizens you attract, the happier you will be.

Happiness is powerful. The wisest humans have already discovered that happier people are healthier, more energetic, less stressed, and more successful. But happiness is much more powerful than that. Happiness is the way that one person in your giant world can change it. One tiny person can impact so many. This is possible because happiness is a cycle that spreads. When you are happy and you cause someone else to be happy, then it makes you happier. The more people you influence to be happy, the more happiness you experience.

There is a saying in your world: "The more you give, the more you receive." It is the same for happiness. The more people you influence to be happy, the more happiness you receive. The cycle continues and spreads until your happiness can affect your entire world.

Happiness first starts with you. Once you are happy, you can spread happiness to your family. Then to your friends. Then to your classmates, then to your teammates, and then to strangers. Can you imagine how many people you can impact? Now imagine if everyone you influenced learned how to train their superhero—then your impact would be unimaginable.

You now know that your happiness starts in your city. Your superhero will defend your Mind Metropolis against bad citizens, but it is your job, in your world, to attract good citizens. Think of your superhero as a defensive player and you, in your world, as an offensive player. Your job is to make good citizens want to come to your city and stay. The way to attract good citizens is to spread happiness in your world.

Dr. RJ and I love smiles. Did you know smiles are contagious? Try smiling at a stranger and see what happens.

Smiles make us feel happy. In fact, smiling is one of the easiest ways to spread happiness. Doing a good deed is another way to spread happiness. If you hold the door for someone, you spread happiness. If you give someone a compliment, you spread happiness. Giving gifts, helping a classmate, and doing chores before your parents ask are all ways to spread happiness. When you spread happiness in your world, you attract good citizens to your Mind Metropolis. When you cause someone else to be happy, in turn you will be happy. It is one of the best cycles in life. There are a-billion-times-infinity number of ways that you can spread happiness. (That's superhero math.)

Each human can positively impact another's life in a unique way. We superheroes still scratch our heads as to why so many of your kind try so hard to fit in with the crowd. You are supposed to be different! You are special and unique. You have been given a gift that only you can share with the world. There is only one of you in your world, there is only one of you that has ever existed, and there is only one of you that will ever exist. No one can be you, and you cannot be someone else. Each of you is special. Each of you is amazing. Each of you is powerful. Do not feel overwhelmed by your duty to change your world. Step up to the challenge. After all, you already trained your superhero.

If you want to change your world, first start with a smile.

SUPERHERO WORKOUT #6:

SPREAD HAPPINESS

Each day, do something nice for someone. Make someone feel special. It can be a family member, classmate, teammate, or complete stranger. Each day go out of your way for someone else. Whether it's washing the dishes without your mom asking or buying a friend's lunch. You can support a friend's social media platform. Show a new student around and introduce them to others. Offer to help a teammate with a new technique you learned. Volunteer at a dog shelter. You can come up with a program where kids help the homeless or other groups in need. You and your friends can visit the nursing home.

If you can't think of something to do for someone else, then look at yourself. Think about what would make you happy. Most likely things that make you happy can make other people happy. I bet you love to swim. Well, so does almost every other kid in your school. Invite a new kid to swim with you and your friends. You can impact others in your own special way. Whatever you choose, do something that benefits someone else.

Doing something nice for others is not the hardest part—it's remembering to do it. So set reminders. Set a phone alert or tape a note on your mirror or put one in your pocket or wear something that will remind you every day. Dr. RJ wears tassels. They serve as his reminder.

DOING NICE THINGS FOR OTHERS MAKES YOU HAPPY!

DOC'S EXAMPLE #6

SHARING HAPPINESS
(AND ENCOURAGEMENT)

Dr. RJ gave his patient Michael an invitation to the kids club's annual bowling party. Dr. RJ asked if he was going to bring any of his friends. Michael hesitated and then said he did not have any friends. Dr. RJ could tell that it bothered Michael. So Doc taught him about the power of happiness—how if Michael became happy first, then he could impact others in a positive way, which would make them happy. And the cycle would continue—then Michael would be happy that he helped those others to be happy. He told Michael how this would make his superhero's job a lot easier.

Michael was normally quiet during his appointments. But at the next appointment, he was very talkative. He asked Dr. RJ if there was a limit to how many friends he could bring to the bowling party.

"I want to invite ten friends," he said. Doc was blown away.

"Yes. Please bring all ten," Dr. RJ replied. He was so happy for Michael.

Michael told Dr. RJ how he learned how to train his superhero and that each Monday he gave every student in his class a personalized note with words of encouragement. He became an instant hit in his class. Several of his classmates started to feel happier Monday mornings. He was so quiet that many did not know him before. Now, after talking more with his classmates, they got a chance to actually know Michael. Many were shocked that he was not the shy, quiet type they thought. Michael loved to talk. Michael learned the impact of making others happy.

CHAPTER 12

FORM A TEAM

What do the Avengers, the X-Men, the Justice League, and the Fantastic Four all have in common? They are all trained superheroes, and they all have a desire to positively impact the world. Sure, Superman was able to do good things by himself, but look at his level of impact once he teamed up with the Justice League.

Now you have trained your superhero. You will change your world by spreading happiness, but imagine the impact if you were to form a team like the Avengers. Imagine if you and all of your friends joined forces to spread happiness in your world.

It's easy to form a superhero team. All you need to do is help your friends train their superheroes. That's all. Once their superheroes are trained, then you can form your own team. What will you name your superhero team? Doc's team is named the SmileInOut Alliance.

Once your team is formed, you can plan your secret meetings. You should meet once a week, once a month, or twice a month. These superhero mastermind meetings should have two main objectives:

1. Discuss strategies to defeat the villains that are attacking your Mind Metropolises.
2. Brainstorm creative ways to spread happiness.

Not only will you and your friends become closer, but your team will be able to achieve a level of change in your world that would not be possible individually.

These secret meetings will help you and your friends overcome common problems that most people face. What makes this meeting different from the other times you and your friends hang out is that you have a specific goal. When you and your friends get together, you probably do it to have fun. At these superhero mastermind meetings, you set aside time to talk about what causes your unhappiness—and how your superheroes might help you be happier. You might want to talk about parents, siblings, your attitude at school, feeling left out, or anything else that you're struggling with.

It is best to have these meetings at least once a month for about fifteen to thirty minutes. Each meeting, your team should choose a topic that works for your group. Take turns, one topic per meeting. If it's your turn to lead, share your feelings around the topic. The other team members will listen (listening is the most important step) and then brainstorm together about different ways to help your superhero deal with the bad citizens who are causing your bad feelings. If you feel sad or disappointed, your thoughts are the cause. So the team will work together to change your thoughts to helpful, positive ones. Once your thoughts are changed, then your feelings will change, and then your actions will change.

After your brainstorming session, spend the rest of your time together in the meeting thinking of ways to spread happiness. A team effort will have more impact than if you were to do it alone. You will be amazed by the ideas your team will come up with to change the world.

DOC'S EXAMPLE #7

TOP SECRET!

All of Dr. RJ's assistants lined up in the hallway to chant Ethan's name because today was the big day. Ethan got his braces off. The patient and his parents were so excited. Ethan high-fived the assistants, and Dr. RJ was waiting with a bag full of taffy, popcorn, and a delicious candied apple, all of the foods that Ethan could not eat when he wore braces.

Ethan's dad thanked Dr. RJ not only for giving his son a perfect smile but also because Dr. RJ helped Ethan start his first superhero team. Dr. RJ had given Ethan a copy of *How to Train Your Superhero* a month before. Once Ethan learned how to train his superhero, he taught his friends from hockey: Ryan, Alexa, Michelle, and Karen. They called themselves the Happy Pucks. They started meeting every Thursday for thirty minutes after hockey practice. Their parents were so happy about their meetings, they bought them pizza for each one.

"How are your superhero mastermind meetings going?" Dr. RJ whispered to Ethan.

"It's going great," Ethan replied quietly.

"Yeah, it is going really well. Last week they talked about ways to stay motivated to finish their homework on time," Ethan's dad said loudly.

Dr. RJ and Ethan both immediately said, "Shhhhhh!"

"Those are secret meetings, Dad," Ethan reminded him.

They all laughed. Ethan left the office wearing a big grin because he was going to change the world while showing off his new smile.

Well, my friend, this is where we part ways.

You have trained your superhero very well. I'm proud of you. I feel confident that your Mind Metropolis is in good hands. Remember everything you have learned and train daily. Remember to pay attention to your citizens. Remember to identify the strategies of the villains. Remember to practice how to defeat your villain. Remember to spread happiness.

Until we meet again, protect your citizens, protect your city, and unleash the power of happiness.

Oh, and make sure you wear your retainer.

ACKNOWLEDGMENTS

First and foremost, all praise and glory goes to my Father in Heaven, and Yeshua (Jesus), His son.

Next, I want to thank the most important woman in this world to me, my wife, Frances. You are truly amazing! Thank you for reading this book over a hundred times. Thank you for all the conversations discussing ideas, and thank you for giving me the thousand + hours to write while you took care of our boys. You are truly a superwoman.

Jeremiah and Isaiah, my sons, I want to thank you for inspiring me each and every day. When I look at you two, it reminds me that God has a bigger plan for my life. Thank you, Mama, for your unwavering encouragement. Anytime I had doubts, you constantly reminded me, "all in God's time."

A special thanks to my sister, Lishawa, for motivating me to start writing again and to finish this book after a two-year delay.

Finally, I want to thank Tegan, for turning my words into a masterpiece. You are very skilled in your abilities and such a joy to work with.

ABOUT THE AUTHOR

Dr. RJ Jackson is an orthodontist and is certified by the Institute for Professional Excellence in Coaching as a life coach for teenagers. He's spent his career working with young people and encouraging them to strive toward good health and happiness. His passion is helping teenagers pursue and achieve their hopes and dreams. Dr. RJ lives and works in Austin, Texas, where you can find him creating smiles on the inside and on the outside. *How to Train Your Superhero* is his first book.

Made in the USA
Monee, IL
28 May 2021